THE TREE IN THE FAR PASTURE

THE TREE
IN THE
FAR PASTURE

by
Sam Ragan

JOHN F. BLAIR, *Publisher*
WINSTON-SALEM
1964

To

MARJORIE
NANCY
TALMADGE

Yes

ON A TIGHT ROPE WITH WILLIAM FAULKNER

There are some kinds of writing,
Malcolm Cowley quotes William Faulkner as saying,
That have to be done very fast
Like riding a bicycle on a tight rope.

And sometimes there are crowds below
To cheer and clap, the echoes
Bouncing from the tent's top.

But many times there is nothing below,
Just sawdust on the floor,
And sometimes in the throat.

Contents

THREE

I

Birth and death and in between
A little living

PORTRAIT

She spoke of things of long ago—
They were as yesterday.
She told of a dream:
It was a September
And it was not really warm until noon.
I had been sitting in the sun, she said.
I could hear a crow across the field.
On the trellis there were new roses.
    I was sitting in the sun,
    And he brought me three fresh pears
        from the tree in the far pasture.

AN OLD LADY SITS BY THE WINDOW AND KNITS

Esoterically speaking,
Shadows decline
Casting pale shadows
On pale hands
That move in and out,
Saying with sad finality,
All is finished.
And yet hoping, as the eyes speak,
Watching glittering goldfish
Swim languidly in the sun.

A COUNTRY SAGA

They carried him home in late August,
And all through the warm days of September
He lay with two broken legs.
Then with the cool nights of October
Came the fever,
And in the haze of the autumn he died.

They buried him in the weed-grown graveyard,
While his father hobbled, dry-eyed, to gaze.
The next day they turned his bed to the sun,
And the smoke of the evening came home to rest.
The old man sat on the porch and smoked.
"It will rain tonight," he said.

"THE PROPHET"

He has grown quieter now,
And almost forgotten—
The Prophet
Only comes to town at tobacco-market time,
And he's only moved to preach
When pimply-faced boys snicker
At his long grey beard and high black hat.
He'll roar at them then,
Damnation and spittle directed at their faces.

But there was a time—yes, there was a time—
When they would not have laughed.
There was a time when he stood in the street
With eyes lifted to an August sun
And hellfire pouring from his lips,
Throwing their sins out for all to see.
The poor bastards who felt that hell could be no hotter
Than the tobacco rows down which they marched—
But sin was real and damnation sure,
And the Prophet knew where to hit them where it hurt.
He could preach for an hour, two hours, and they
        would listen,
Scuffing the dirt and never hunting shade
Until the Prophet had poured out his scorn
And walked away.

The old man's fire is gone now.
He dozes in the shade of a mulberry tree
And mumbles to himself, brushing flies from his face—
Hell is far away,
Beyond the cornfield, the cotton patch,
And maybe even beyond the dusty towns of long ago.

DESERTED HOUSE

He went out at dusk,
    out from the house
That stood beyond the little patch
    of pine, where honeysuckle
    grew along the ground, and a large boulder
    reared, and around it
    the path circled.
He went out at dusk,
    and there was a whippoorwill's cry
From the dark wood and across the fields
    now broken with October.
Somewhere . . . somewhere. He did not know. . . .
And the woman who saw him go
Knew that he would not be back.
She left the door open
    and night crept in,
    and when she had gone,
    how many days, weeks, or months had gone by. . . .
The sunlight slanted across the floor
And a curious squirrel left tracks in the dust.

NEIGHBORS

I imagine he got rather lonely
Living that far from town
With no neighbors close enough
To drop by at night for a smoke and talk.
And living alone gives time for too much thought—
It's that way especially at night.

The time I saw him he was standing in front
Of his little house on the hill
Watching our train as it passed by.
He waved at us
And I fancy that meant something to him—
Waving at the train as it passed each day.
It was morning then and the man probably
Spent the rest of the day walking
Under the trees around his house.

But at night he doesn't have much
Except the wind to listen to
And a fire to nurse along
Until it's time to go to bed.
In the morning he can watch for the train
And wave at us as we go by.

MAN IN TIME

He was afraid of storms
    and hid in culverts or potato houses
    when they came in.
Sometimes he grew a beard,
    in sumertime, too—a red beard—
    and he would not wash,
    and went for weeks without talking.
Once I saw him plowing past midnight
    in a full moon,
    crying out at the far turn
    to a sleepy horse
    that stumbled in the dark—
    strange sounds of gee, haw and goddamn
    in broken words across broken ground.
Then he would be gone
    in polished shoes, shaven,
    and wearing a panama hat.
No word for days.
And then smoke from the chimney
    and wild curses for the cat, for the dog, the land,
    and for the man.

HOME IS THE HUNTER

He stares from a window in a darkened room
At moonrise over hills where
The full cry of hounds is heard.
His fingers smooth the warm cane wood
As shadows play across floor and face.
His ear follows the fading hunt
Beyond the woods, under silent stars.

He sits alone.
    A dog barks in a distant yard.
    A night bird calls,
    And the cricket resumes his cry.

TWO

In the old house they sit alone—
    The rain in the trees
    Is hidden by darkness.
And hidden, too, are hoarded griefs
Forgotten now as to why or how.
    Still—
    Silent faces turn
    To a watchful clock,
    Crying to time:
Tell me, tell me.

A DANCE AND DEATH FROM MY WINDOW

It was a little dance before death
On the stone steps of an April morning.
I saw him from the window—
A swinging of arms, and then the quick jig.
The days were few and then the wreath
Hung on the door.
A man brought flowers and she stood weeping,
He twisting his hat in his hands,
And she dabbing at eyes,
Saying something I could not hear.
Some rites the dead demand,
And they were done.
The street was quiet again—
The lilac bloomed.
And on a lazy afternoon
A long lean cat stalked
A singing bird.

POSTWAR

He came home from Petersburg,
Footing it down the road with three others
Who fell off by the way,
He going the last miles alone.
The chimney's smoke quickened his steps.
She was waiting in the doorway
And ran down the path to meet him.
Not much was said:
They walked back together
And he took off his hat and stood a moment
Before going in to supper.

He cleaned the spring,
And there were three places in the fence to mend.
A new ground was cleared,
And after the plowing was done,
Along the road he planted a row of cedars.

THE FALLS OF NEUSE

Where the water rushes white over the rocks
He had squatted and made signs
Over a pine-knot fire,
Drawing circles in spots of scuffed-out clay.
Lawson marked it on his maps.

The boy with the blue eyes
Went down in the second round,
But golden dreams and Golden Gloves
Babbled forth as he clawed at his hair. . . .
Losers can't go home—
What would he tell them at the company store?

The mill on the Neuse has been quiet a long time now,
Honeysuckle has climbed the fence,
And weeds grow in the yard.
But they still talk of the cotton-headed boy
Who got up off the floor and went on,
Taking his licks and giving more.
"He was a good 'un," they say.
Lawson?
"He musta moved away when the shutdown come."

WILLIE JONES

A midnight grave, and a hundred seekers since—
What matters the burial place,
Or was it the final twisted grin
Of the broadcloth man
Asserting his identity?

That time in Hillsborough
When he held back till
The words were put down,
Garlands of guarantees for every man—
They would remember that.

The burial pair held their tongue
And the rains of Raleigh soon conspired
With falling leaves and wind to hide
The final home and haven . . .
But there are seekers still.

LINCOLN MEMORIAL

The cars go around it
To get on to Constitution Avenue,
And you have to watch out
To keep from hitting
Children with boxes of popcorn,
Men with cameras,
And old ladies in print dresses
Who walk on flat feet.

They come from everywhere
And sometimes you can see their faces
In the reflecting pool,
Toward which he sits and stares
With eyes of bronze.

FLANNERY O'CONNOR

. . . the peacocks cry all night long: help me, help me.

Four miles from Milledgeville on a farm
Of five hundred acres
She raised chickens (and peacocks).

She talked of grotesques,
Southern style—of freaks who felt
The call to preach,
Of praying violent men with something
In the blood driving them
Onward but inward.

Broiler prices had been falling,
And it had not rained for weeks.
The grass was almost gone in the pastures.
There had been a fire,
But the damage was slight.

She held their attention
With strong Georgia phrases
Drawing pictures of a people
In a land all their own, shifting
Suddenly from darkness to hard sunlight,
Caught in the giant hands of fate and the will of God.
        But the violent bear it away.
        And a good man is hard to find.

The crutches lean against the wall
Unnoticed and forgotten.

In the shade of the trees
The peacocks strut.

But at night in the mellow darkness
They cry . . .
All night long . . .
Help me.
Help me.

THE MONUMENT ON THE CAPITOL GROUNDS

He leans forward, gun in hand,
Stone eyes staring, forelock falling
Over forehead on which a pigeon sat.
    First to fall at Bethel,
    The stone words say . . .
But that was long ago
In a little churchyard
Where bullets whined, and where
A dog now whimpers
On a rabbit's path.
    And in the square azaleas bloom,
    A girl comes walking . . .
    The stone soldier stares.
    He does not hear the mockingbird's cry.

THE ONE SMALL SINGING

Novelists deal with the time of man—
Birth and death, and in between a little living
That barely breathes and seldom bleeds.
And poets, too, but rarely find
The shining moment
Or the one small singing
Of every man.

II

The beach is a lonely place
On days like this

GRAY HORIZONS

Sometimes the birds pause in flight
To feed upon the foam-beaten sands,
But more often they wheel and cry
Far overhead, never stopping, until night's
Soft crescendo of silence
Calls them home.

The beach is a lonely place
On days like this,
And eyes see far until
The place where sea meets sky
Brings vision back again
To the glitter and cry
Of flashing sea gulls.

And here is the haven of
Life's mute testimonials—
A broken oar, a battered box,
And here the wreckage of some
Mist-shrouded Odyssey.
They tell no tales, except silence:
The story is your own.

THAT DAY ON THE BEACH

The wind came up
And then the rain—
We ran for shelter
And were very wet.
The rain on your face looked like tears,
But you were laughing.

That was long ago, but I remembered it
When I awoke this morning
To a clap of thunder
In the still air of summer.

FLIGHT

The river bends and finds its way
    past the cities,
And the clouds cover the rubbage of wrongs
Hidden in the clots and clusters of houses.
I see the brown fields.

There was frost this morning
When I arose in the late darkness
Searching the shadows of the lawn
For the last scampering of squirrels.
But there were roses blooming—
Rare on these days—
And I could not write the realness of the day
Or speak beyond the silence
Surrounding our thoughts.
We nod in understanding—
Saying
    Good morning, Good morning.

HIDDEN SCARS

Fire had come to these woods one day
    and left the trees blackened and scarred—
    dead in places, too—
    with their limbs hanging like the broken wing of a
        bird.
But they came out of it somehow—
    out of the fire, I mean—
    and five years, ten years, perhaps,
    one would never know of the hidden scars . . .
Unless other fires came.

THE RIVER

The old stern-wheeler has gone up the river
Pushing barges.
They won't be needing her any more.
And she will end her days in drydock.
     But the river laughs.
The river will go on and on and on,
On to the sea.
     And the sea goes on forever.

ON STOPPING BY A DESERTED HOUSE ON A
SUNNY AFTERNOON

We look but do not enter.
The old house is almost gone,
And a man could break a leg
Falling through a rotting board.
Besides, in all those kudzu vines
There's a likely nest
Of copperheads waiting
To sink a fang in flesh
Or at least scare the hell out of you
By their hissing.

LIMITED ACCESS

In time
All the roads become
One big road—
A by-pass that takes you away
From where people are,
And there is no exit
Until the next town.

NOTE TO A PAINTER OF PICTURES ON A
MORNING IN NOVEMBER

A red ladder leans against a white house,
And beyond the trees
Through bare branches
There is blue sky.

WITHIN THE CITY'S SIGHTS

Outside the window the people move
    on frowning streets.
In the park beyond an old man throws peanuts—
    popcorn maybe—
To a squirrel.
The sound of cars and trucks
Drowns out the small cry
Of why.

SANCTUARY

Perhaps, I may say, there was stillness,
And the hem of his robe was purple
Edged in rose, and his eyes
Stared straight ahead.
Flickering candles threw shadows
Over pictures of saints
Burned for believing.
Somewhere an organ played,
But there was no sound
From his measured steps on the red carpet,
A book held to the breast.
Sunlight slanted through the windows,
Catching fixed faces in poses of piety.

IN AN ALL-NIGHT CAFE

He puts the coffee cup before me
And turns to fill the urn again.
While I sip coffee he moves to the end of the counter
And resumes the reading of a newspaper
Printed in Greek.
And when he stops to stare across the room
I fancy he dreams of the time
When he can sell out
And go home again
To that island of ancient stones,
And sun and sea.

FINAL EDITION

They have all gone from the city room.
Down the long hall the last footsteps have died away.
The teletypes are quiet,
But in the distance is the rumble
Of the fresh-inked last news.
The sweeper has come and gone.

A green eyeshade lies on the desk—
    And there's no one to answer the telephone.

III

Feeling and finding words
For April mornings and winter night

A POET IS SOMEBODY WHO FEELS

A poet, said e. e. cummings, is somebody who feels,
   and expresses his feelings through words.
Something that cannot be taught like thinking can,
Something that makes you nobody but yourself.
   Feeling and finding words
   For April mornings and winter night,
   Birds against the sky on October afternoons,
   Old fields and lonely streets,
   Or sunlit days
   When a girl walks by,
   And the heart is crying
   For things that have no names.
   Feeling . . .

Nobody . . .
   Nobody but yourself.

THAT TIME

I come with words at lilac time,
Hunting under leaves for arbutus.
Blue sky and bloom are now in view
As April comes greening.
      And last night
In the last full moon of March
The wind sifted down
The petals of pears.

DAYLIGHT AND DARK

In midsummer heat,
When clouds that promise more wind than rain
Brush against the sky
Beyond the tallest pines,
Take heed of the small desires.
Let the stopper out,
Bit by bit perhaps,
If caution still remains first nature,
Or let it fall
Noiseless to the floor.
For the red sun moves slowly to the west,
Hangs motionless . . . suspended in space . . .
For a moment . . . and then falls
In slowly ebbing light
Before the quiet dark.

SUNDOWN AT TOPSAIL

The strong white dogs of daylight
Run fast
To touch the last rim
Of an ancient sky now filled
With the last low flights
Of gulls crying,
Dipping wings to wave's crest
Before going home.

SEASONS

From dogwood white to dogwood red,
That's the way summer's fled.

THE TILT OF THE FALL

The moon rides high over hunched-up hills,
Dying is September's lot,
Though nights are cool,
Summer is still with us,
And the cricket's last song fills
A night with sound.
This is the balancing time
Of even days and even nights.
The tilt will come with the fall.

NO ONE MOCKS OCTOBER

These cool nights and a clean bright moon
Do not mock blue days of sun
And last bird call.

No one mocks October—
Its innocent blue eyes
Watch death without blinking,
Even the last gasps, and
Lonely walks in stripped fields
With throat so tight you cannot cry.

No one mocks October—
The mockery is its own.

NOTHING IN NOVEMBER

We come to November and open our hands
To nothing.
For what was the long travel
Out of the dark and the fog,
Feeling for handholds
On twisted branches, and
Falling in the holes of burned-out stumps?
Somehow we hovered with time,
Pushing it aside bit by bit
As we would cobwebbed vines.
Now the leaves are gone,
The trees look ancient,
And footsteps are only a shuffle.
What should I say—
The hands clutch only the fog—
And the face is wet as it moves
Toward the light.

44

DEER HUNT

We rode out to the west of town.
It was November, the leaves were brown,
And the wind was pushing against the pines
That stood at the crest of the hill.
We saw it but made no comment.
The deer was motionless,
There by the side of the road.
We had slowed, watching him,
Wondering the way he would go.
There was the shot, he leaped high
And came to rest on the road's edge. . . .
Down the bank scrambled the men,
Guns cradled in their arms,
And they gathered round,
Not too close, they feared his kick. . . .
But he was dead, and soon they lifted him up
To test his size, his weight, to count his points.
We saw instead his glazed eyes,
Remembered him alive as he stood in our view,
And we drove away.

INVENTORY TIME

It was year's end
And the spirals of smoke
Spoke of clear weather—
At least for a few days.
Time to hit the road again
With stories to tell,
Selling things and self.
But this was inventory time:
They would tell him to come back. . . .
Not now—some other time. . . .
And he would close the sample case,
Feeling that small bite in the belly,
But laughing—okay . . . so long . . . see you next time.
    And here in the last single
    With window that looked on a blank wall
    He added up the mileage on the Rambler—
    Maybe time for a trade-in—

Inventory time . . .
    No place to go, no one to call,
        . . . and the fifth's almost gone.

WALKING ON THIS WINTER NIGHT

Walking on this winter night
I count the stars
Through the crook of a tree:
Count them and claim them
As my own.
Each with plan and purpose
Apart from what I see.
But still I can claim them
And make them serve my purpose
On this night of walking.

MOON WATCH

The moon is now above the trees,
The wind has risen and the rain is gone.
    I stand at the window.
I feel the darkness in the shadows,
The darkness within me—
    Where did you go?

I hear footsteps but I see no one.
The moon does not tell me.
    And I, at the window, can only guess—
    Why and when and where?
The moon moves on in a racing sky,
And I stand watch in a darkened room.
    Will you come back?

SHADOWS

I walk in the shadows
   . . . I walk in the shadows
   of the fence that encloses me;
I walk in the shadows of your face.

    The wistaria of time entwines me.
    I see the moon through the frothy leaves,
    The shadows play tricks,
    And I see you dancing.

There are pathways that give no sound to the feet,
No trace of steps taken.
The shadows have hidden them
In the movement of moonlight.

    I walk in the shadows—
       . . . the shadows of your face.

THE MIND'S CORRAL

In the fury and the frenzy
Of the mind's small corral
They run in small circles,
Close to the fence, but never looking over,
Or beyond . . . always in the dusty tracks
Of yesterday and the day before.
Time's little grooves are magnetized
To hold iron hooves in round gallops
Once, twice, three times . . .
Before the stumbling fall
In the wind-stirred dust.

A THING OF CRYING WINGS

In this small circle of light
We bring together the unsaid things
Of wonder and hope that lie beyond
The haze of horizons.
Groping for words
Hovering in the shadows
Of the heart, crying
There is no time . . . no time.
 And repeating what the poet asked:
 Why is my love always a thing of crying wings?

TRAVELER TO A TIME OF LILACS

You ask where I have been—
        I do not know.
But yesterday across the sky
I broke the sound barrier.
My sky was a place of sun and silence.

My thoughts were of the whisper of trees,
And the frog's first cry
In a lilac night.

PLUMS

The plums you brought to me
In your hands
Had on them a smokiness—
Faint wisps of purple
And curls of blue.

THE CALL

The voices kept saying,
Come on, come on.
And the walk went through the valleys,
Sometimes the hills.